Peter Kakos

LAST BLUE

LAST BLUE

Poems

GERALD STERN

W. W. Norton & Company New York • London

Poems in this volume have appeared or will appear in the following journals:
The American Poetry Review: "Pluma," "Domestic," "Greek Neighbor Home
from the Hospital," "Lavender," "Short Words," "The Music," "Night,"
"Mexican," "Drowning on the Pamet River," "Art," "Paris," "Already April,"
"The Dove's Neck," "Sleep," "August 20–21," "This Life," "Last Blue,"
"Kingdom"; *Doubletake:* "Massachusetts Song"; *Exquisite Corpse:* "The
Sorrows"; *Field:* "Progress and Poverty"; *Gettysburg Review:* "Old Scarf"; *Iowa
Review:* "Wailing"; *New Yorker:* "March 27"; *New York Times:* "Dirty Hands";
Ploughshares: "Against the Crusades," "An Explanation"; *Poetry:* "Pamet
Harbor," "Someone to Watch Over Me," "Visiting My Own House in Iowa
City," "Big Annie Rooney," "Scratch," "Swifts," "Ravages"; *Slate:* "Forsythia,"
"Larry Levis Visits Easton, Pa. During a November Freeze," "Pennsylvania
Bio," "A Separate Logic"; *TriQuarterly:* "Kingdom"; *Yale Review:* "Which One?"

For information about permission to reproduce selections from this book,
write to Permissions, W. W. Norton & Company, Inc., 500 Fifth Avenue,
New York, NY 10110

The text and display type of this book are composed in Perpetua
Composition by Matrix Publishing Services
Manufacturing by Courier Companies, Inc.
Book design by Chris Welch

Library of Congress Cataloging-in-Publication Data
Stern, Gerald, 1925–
    Last blue : poems / Gerald Stern.
        p. cm.
    ISBN 0-393-04897-7
     I. Title.
    PS3569.T3888 L37 2000
    811'.54—dc21   99-055508

W. W. Norton & Company, Inc., 500 Fifth Avenue, New York, N.Y. 10110
www.wwnorton.com

W. W. Norton & Company, Ltd., 10 Coptic Street, London WC1A 1PU

1 2 3 4 5 6 7 8 9 0

For Anne Marie

CONTENTS

I

II

III

IV

V

VI

I

ONE OF THE SMALLEST

Made of the first gray light
that came into my room,
made of the hole itself
in the cracked window blind,
thus made of sunshine, thus made of
gas and water, one of the
smallest, smallest, made of
that which seizes the eye,
that which an eagle needs
and even a mole, a mole, a
rabbit, a quail, a lilac,
it was uncreated. I
fought for it, I tore down
walls, I cut my trees,
I lay on my back, I had a
rock to support my head, I
swam in two directions,
I lay down smiling, the sun
made my eyes water, what
the wind and the dirt took away
and what was abraded and what was
exhausted, exhausted, was only
a just reflection. The sun
slowly died and I much
quicker, much quicker, I raced
until I was wrinkled but I was
lost as the star was and I
was losing light, I was dying
before I was born, thus I was
blue at the start, though I was

red much later, much later,
for I was a copy, but I was
something exploding and I was
born for just that but fought
against it, against it. The light
of morning was gray with a green
and that of evening was almost a
rose in one sky though it was
white in another—at least
in one place the light comes back—
and I disappeared like a fragment
of gas you'd call it, or fire,
fragment by fragment I think,
cooled down and changed into metal,
captured and packaged as it will be
in one or two more centuries
and turned then into a bell—
not a bridge, not a hammer—
really the tongue of a bell,
if bells will still be in use then,
and I will sing as a bell does,
you'd call it tolling—such
was my burst of light seen from
a certain viewpoint though seen from
another, another, no sudden
flash but a long slow burning
as in the olive tree burning,
as in the carob, as slow as the
olive, still giving up chocolate
after two thousand years, that's
what we lacked, our light
was like the comet's, like a
flash of fosfur, a burst
from a Spanish matchbox, the wood

broken in two, the flame
lasting six seconds—I counted—
that is, when the fosfur worked,
two or three lives lived out
in a metal ash tray, one of them
nothing but carbon, one of them
wood part way, poor thing that
died betimes, one snuffed out
just at the neck where the pinkish
head was twisted the wrong way
and one of them curling up
even after burning, thus the
light I loved stacked in a box
depending on two rough sides
and on the wind and on the
gentleness of my hand,
the index finger pressed
against the wood, the flash
of fire always a shock,
always new and enlightening,
the same explosion forever—
I call it forever—forever—
sitting with my mouth open
in some unbearable blue,
bridal wreath in my right hand,
since this is the season, my left hand
scratching and scratching, the sun
in front now. How did dogwood
get into this yard? How did
the iris manage to get here?
And grow that way? I live
without a beard, I'm streaked
with a kind of purple, my hands
are folded and overlapping, I

love the rain, I am
a type of Persian, where I am
and in this season I blossom
for fifteen hours a day, I
walk through streams of some sort—
I like that thinking—corpuscles
bombard my eyes—I call it
light—it was what gave me
life in the first place—no no
shame in wandering, no shame
in adoring—what it what it
was was so primitive
we had to disturb it—call it
disturbing, call it interfering—
at five in the morning in front of
the dumpster, at six looking down
on the river, a little tired from
the two hundred steps, my iris
in bloom down there, my maples
blowing a little, I was
a mole and a rabbit, I was
a stone at first, I turned
garish for a while and burned.

*The name
of Light
is Love

16

II

PLUMA

Once, when there were no riches, somewhere in southern
Mexico I lost my only pen in the
middle of one of my dark and flashy moments
and euchered the desk clerk of my small hotel
out of his only piece of bright equipment
in an extravagance of double-dealing,
nor can I explain the joy in that and how I
wrote for my life, though unacknowledged, and clearly
it was unimportant and I had the money and
all I had to do was look up the Spanish and
I was not for a second constrained and there was
no glory, not for a second, it had nothing to
do with the price of the room, for example, it only
made writing what it should be and the life we
led more rare than what we thought and tested
the art of giving back, and some place near me,
as if there had to be a celebration
to balance out the act of chicanery,
a dog had started to bark and lights were burning.

PAMET HARBOR

Going west to east on the Pamet River I sang
in the wet grasses though I was hardly dismembered
and as far as I could tell neither Christ nor Apollo
was shutting poets up. In fact, I played
my favorite tape while Haba was pulling weeds
out of the motor: "A Kiss to Build a Dream On,"
and "Sweet Lorraine" and "Makin' Whoopee," the voice
the one we adored, that wise throatiness—
Apollo couldn't do that—nor the eyeballs
nor the thick lips, the light so brilliant it shone
on all of us, we had to look at the sky;
and the wrinkled smile—Apollo just couldn't do that
with wings alone (though Christ could!) makin' whoopee.

AGAINST THE CRUSADES

Don't think that being a left-handed nightingale was all
   legerdemain
or that I am that small angry bastard who hates whores,
only I disguised it by laughing; or that it's
easy leaving a restaurant by yourself and holding
your other hand against the bricks to keep from falling;
or anybody can play the harp, or anybody knows the words
to Blue Sunday and After the Ball Was Just Over You Dropped
   Dead.

If you can stand Strauss then so can I,
oh filthy Danube, oh filthy Delaware, oh filthy Allegheny.

And anyone who never opened a Murphy bed
night after night for seven years without ripping
the sheet and had neither desk nor dresser can't walk
in my shoes or wear my crocodile T-shirt.
And anyone thinking that a Jew being a Jew
is something you should apologize for as if Richard
Wagner just stepped into the room wearing a bronze
headpiece with a pink feather sticking out of it
is nothing less than a fool himself who buys into
dead stoves and dead feelings and doesn't know the
sweetness of his own lips and the tenderness of his fingers.

God bless the Jewish comedians who never denigrated Blacks,
and God bless the good gentiles and God bless Mayor Scully
and Councilman Wolk and Rosie Rosewall and Eleanor
   Roosevelt;
and the chorus of Blue Saints behind Bishop Elder Beck

and the old theater on Wylie Avenue I visited every Sunday
    night
to hear them sing and pray and hear him preach.

God bless the Lucca Cafe. God bless the green benches
in Father Demo Square and the dear Italian lady
carrying a huge bouquet of red and white roses
in front of her like a candelabra and the tiny white
baby's breath that filled the empty spaces with clapping and
    singing.

RAVAGES

I hold my right hand up so the Greek will stop
talking for a minute; I am recording
everything with my left and my wrist is hurting
as it always does. His harsh language
is a combination of anger and humor, one
supporting the other, and his body, stiff
and out of control, is just an extension of
his scattered words. His wife went to the Poconos
to be with their oldest daughter for a while
and he is rebuffed and lonely so he talks
to a dove and reads his paper. He it was who
cursed the Colonels and he it was who slept
in a cave in 1942 and fought
the Germans with a hunting rifle, he tied
a knife blade to the bore, and suffered indignities
selling hot dogs in Easton, Pennsylvania,
for twenty years and he deserves some love.
He lifts himself with a twirling motion and when he
reaches into my yard to steal a tea rose
I tell him—in English—how the leg has to breathe;
and how the forehead absorbs the sun. I kick
my watering can so he kicks his and we slam
our kitchen doors together though his was a second
after mine, or mine after his, so one of us
is left alone and one turns on his light
before the other does and starts his tea
a second sooner or closes his bedroom window
before the other or studies his ravages.

WHATEVER PARIS MEANT

It wasn't till Monday, November 14, 1994
that I decided Offenbach was too glutted
and the oompah-pah would have to go,
though sometimes my mood changed
and all the spitefulness of that half-century
was converted to the pleasure of understanding,
the oh-yes and ah-yes I learned in my first ten years
behind two pillars and a roomful of starched curtains.

Whatever Paris meant in 1950,
whatever of Gide was in the air
and pitched battles over Coca-Cola
and the wearing of black behind a piece of horse meat,
there still was enough, thanks God, of the bella, bella,
to last a few more years.
                              And there was a man
who carried a leather bag of small red Bibles—
he was our personal fury and stood over us
singing *jeunesse passe* and *jeunesse passe,*
something between a crow and a sparrow. It was
our cry for over a year, it was the greeting
between us. Once at three in the morning
when my Rumanians woke me up for soup
we pounded each other on the bridge going over
and sang it in French and German. Something of Offenbach
was in our hearts; we jumped up on the rails
and fell to the sidewalk on our knees; we did it
all night.
                  In the morning when I wrote
and waited for my Briton to make my bed

so I could bend over her, I wiped those drums out
and buried those Rumanians. I didn't know
about sighing yet; I just stared at the fixture
and she fell asleep with her hand on my shoulder. I walk
with my two arms waving sometimes; I am explaining,
and I have the limp I started in Paris, a kind of
rolling from side to side. I still crash into
male and female hydrants. I still lean
against the metal poles to stretch my hamstrings,
and I still do a dream-walk from one end
of New York to the other, west to east
and south to north.
                    The music goes
oompah, oompah, oompah, the words
are *jeunesse passe* and *jeunesse passe*; the window
faced a Moroccan smoke shop, the street was empty.

SOMEONE TO WATCH OVER ME

It is not knowing what a mulberry sidewalk looks like
in the first place that will start you up sliding, then dancing,
though if it weren't for my bird-like interior and how I shake
one foot then the other I would have not seen the encroachment
myself; and if it weren't for the squirrel who lives in pure greed
and balances whatever he touches with one hand then another
I would have picked the berries up one berry at a time
and laid them out to dry beside my crinkled lily and my pink
    daisy.
In this decade I am taking care of the things I love. I'm
sorting everything out starting, if I have to, with the
smallest blossom, the smallest, say, salmon-colored petunia.
I'm eating slowly, dipping one crumb at a time in my beer,
and singing—as I never did before—one word at a time
in my true voice, which is after all a quiet second tenor
that came upon me after my first descent into manhood
and after a disgrace involving my seventh grade music teacher
and a sudden growth of hair. If it weren't for my large lips
I could have played the French horn. If I didn't like
    mulberries—
one among a million, I know, and eat them—without sugar—
the way a grackle does his from the downtrodden branches
I wouldn't be standing on a broken chair, and I wouldn't be
    shaking;
and if I didn't slide from place to place and walk
with a toothbrush in my pocket and touch one bush
for belief and one for just beauty I wouldn't be singing.

WAILING

Walking from west to east past the living
dead man on the corner of Grove and Fourth
north side of the bank I closed my eyes
so I wouldn't have to see his stumps and the red
mouth without a tongue and make the water
rush through my ears so I wouldn't have to hear him.

And sitting on the bench across the street
I exchanged ideas with the woman next to me
on a question in ethics, Kant and Schlegel; I made
a reference to early Herodotus, she stuck by
Bentham, pleasure and pain, though she was loyal
also to Hobbes, he of the loathsome universe.

While the sun, though who would notice it, was covered
in what the older Plato would call slime
and the one tree that didn't have metal growing
through it shook with life—I'd say it was leaves
but birds rushed by and one was Bentham and one
was Hobbes himself, one of the true slime-chasers.

And sitting across from me although the lice
drove him crazy was the master of nuance
lifting a wing and eating, he of the blinking
eyes we waited for standing alone
and walking along the slats of his bench, the prince
of bleeding mouths, I'm sure, and duke of welts,

not to mention organs erupting and faces
some black and some red but all with huge creases and I,
with a scholar like that, I kept him in bread, I gave him
one Guggenheim after another, even I
gave him a Hobbes, a half a bagel, with seeds
from the opium tree and did my drumming, hands

on the cement armrests, now beginning to clap,
and a tongue of my own inside my mouth, still thinking,
still talking, I will learn to forgive, still lucky
to have a tongue and sit in New York and bleed
only a little, from one or two cuts, and lucky
to walk the way I do and have my own secret

and shoulder my bag as I get up and walk
to another part of the city, past, I'm sure,
shoes and wine and futons, thinking up
a plan for not eating, a place for my papers, a room
to read in, a chair to live in my next two years
and keep my tongue intact, poor suffering mouth

at the corner of Fourth and Grove, and lie down hard
when I have to and sit where I want and wait for my own
restaurant to open and drink my coffee at last
in a certain park, at another bench, this one
with curved iron sides in stamped black: fruit and flowers
and yellow lacquered slats, a bench for wailing,

with a name on it in English and even dates
for someone to study and only three short lines
to memorize, the plate attached with bolts
from front to back, the metal treated, a rat
for witness, a sparrow to eat the pizza, a *Times*
to sit on, a daughter for whistling, a mother for staring,

and someone to loosen the bolts and someone to stand
in front of me with a flute and throw his hat
on a little Turkish rug and someone to sit
beside me and wail, "coffee from 1940,"
"pie from 1936," the only
song I know, half Mississippi, half Poland.

The difference between my house in Pennsylvania
and my house in Massachusetts is the difference between
fish stinking in one place and birds in the other.
The dead and bygone locusts in both places attest to this,
and the salt water bringing the sea back into my inland river.
Suffering being equal, I am happy for the three berries
on the high bush and the mullein sticking out like
swollen asparagus in the sand and grass of Fisher Road.
Basic fruit is what I got, an apple
red as fire on one side, soft and wormy
on the other, something like dew for polish, something
like crapulous breasts, like bulbous bleeding lips.
And eating is what I did, my teeth and tongue
nibbling and sucking as if I were cross-legged still,
as if I had lifted my left hand up and killed
a dragonfly. Both places are edged with phlox
but the water—and the sky—are different. That is why
the currents I moved in were so different and why,
though I started off as one thing, I ended up
as something else. The water took me down
a slice or two. I have become what I was.
Some storm or other changed one thing into another.
You could say that the ocean broke through and what was
fresh water with frogs and lilies and cattails became
much sparser and bleaker, you could say unprotected,
or there was danger and no one knew who had
authority or there was a mix now of salt
and fresh in the mouths of rivers and this was only
transition, and let it go at that. Seen from
above and beyond, out of hearing—and sight—

I could go back *or* forth. Honor and love
to *both* those things. Or I could join one hand
to the other. I used to say "one foot," I said
a river, I said a heart; my brain in the marsh
knows both those things, my freshwater brain, my brain
of pity and fear and cunning, my brain of laughter,
my lung of desperation—seawater lung—
brackish liver—seaweed stomach—
and skin of pain and skin of adventure and skin
of perfect love and peeling skin and skin of
filth and disgrace, my drum, my lampshade, skin
of water sloshing back and forth, the left hand
brine, the right hand alkaline, the sulphur,
the hard, the soft, the chlorine, the spring, glossy
pokeweed of Millpond Road, long dry grasses of Fisher.

WHICH ONE?

In Memory of James Merrill

I should wait to see if the dog goes first or the tree
and when that sky turns red which one will pull me
into the street and if I set up my table
should I face the burnt-out windows or the cornfield.

The teeth are the same and only the clump of green grass
growing in the fork instead of the bony forehead
makes the difference, and if one bends down to howl
what does it matter the flesh or the woolen branches.

The paint went first and after that the doors
and after that I turned to my curled geranium,
buried as it was in clay and washed the deer off,
licking her baby and washed the forest. Life

goes on and on—a chair at the table, a long
white curtain, a pen that works. I kiss a leaf—
like that—I start my sweeping, I pick up a kind
of goblet for drinking, I break a burned glass for love.

A SEPARATE LOGIC

All he had to know was that the rails
went one way and the highway went another
and that there was a separate logic, something
he didn't have to understand; the lakes
anyhow kept him busy and straining to hear
the French in front of him. General Motors,
he tried to explain, destroyed the beds, but they
were only interested in the foliage. One thing
he learned about the Swiss, they ate all morning
and talked without a letup, and they liked
our lakes as much as theirs. Sometimes the rails
followed the road, or vice versa, horses
versus horses; where he sat the sun
shone behind the trees, he caught the trunks
and most of the branches; he was at peace because
he could hate the corporations and still
adore the leaves; he learned to do that in Pittsburgh,
studying Frick then walking through the woods
and loving the hills and looking down, nothing
gave him greater pleasure, finding a marble
hoof, for example, or a seashell, in some
remote Pennsylvania park, or in a factory
given over to profit to see a doorknob
made, as it were, in Crete, or China. He crushed
his cup in the netting as they moved over
water, "he was at sea," he said to the Swiss
and he explained how "money talked" just as they
climbed through another woods. He was hoping
a small leaf would stick to the window, something
red, with a pear to match, a Bartlett; pears

and apples made him sleep. There was one bridge
diagonally under another, they were flying
into and through each other; there were two leaves,
one on top of the other and it was raining.

VISITING MY OWN HOUSE
IN IOWA CITY

The three large dogs in my house
scraping and sliding on the wood
and running from window to window
reminded me of the enraged
three-headed dog from Hell,
yet one of them was only
a flat-coated black retriever
and one was only a coonhound
and one was a loving golden mixture
with a large trusting muzzle. They
belonged to my friend Mark Doty
who with his partner Paul
was renting the house but they
were away when I rang the bell;
knowing this made me human,
knowing they were just pets,
and when I went to the backyard
and saw my weeping willow had toppled,
although I wavered a little
at the crude aggrandisement
and almost hung a dead flower
on a piece of the orange wood
in memory of my thirteen years
away from New York and Pennsylvania
I came out to the sidewalk
more chastened than I was bitter;
and living with that I drove
back to my hotel room
to watch the telephone blinking

and then to sleep the sleep
of the consigned and forgotten, ice
covering my eyeballs, for example,
rainwater engorging my heart,
before I ate my supper
in a vat of grease, the pig
I came there to bless, the corn
I came to transform and to love.

DOMESTIC

He picked a leaf, there just had to be
a little drama wherever he went, he put it
in the left pocket with the number two pencil
and the set of keys; it was a little wet,
which made it diaphanous, and when he pressed it
inside his book, although it had started to dry
and even shrink, it still could be supple and even
give off a little knowledge. Halfway across
to his second house he held it in his mouth
the way an ape does; this was another drama
and he wasn't even accountable; the taste
was nothing, only looking for his keys
he swallowed a little juice. Where he put it
down and how he looked at it later when
he walked out for his oranges he would remember
while sitting beside his lamp with a paper napkin
under his coffee and eating a little and turning
the light into the wall, the heavy stem
like a trunk, the branches upturned, the stunted ones,
as in all leaves half-glistening, a tree
that lived on a blue rug and curled and rose
for its deathbed speech he swept up or he scattered.

BIG ANNIE ROONEY

Counting the beats in a different way he used
the round white doily for a drum; he kept
his right hand in the air half conducting
and smashed a finger or two on the hard maple
under the captain's lamp with the fake wick
in the fake lighthouse window on the fake metal base.
He could see it was going to be a struggle
between his Big Bill Broonzy and his Big John Cage,
and he sang them both—although you wouldn't call
what he did with Cage was singing. It had to
do with breath, certainly not with the silence
and not with the sound and not with the agony,
though both of them probably missed their mother's houses,
if they reflected on it in different ways,
and both of them are dead. He touched two buttons,
one for wind and one for rain. He waited
the twilight out an hour or so and even
resisted turning the light on so he could see
the difference between the two kinds of darkness
without interference. He rested his left wrist
where the throbbing had started. He rubbed his broken knuckles
with Dr.'s Cream and warmed up the other hand,
the lookalike, the goody-goody, the raise
your right hand swear, the wooden ruler, the metal
edge, Miss Donaldson's ruler, Miss Black's, the nervous
blinking, the subversion, Big Bill Broonzy, Big Annie Rooney.

SCRATCH

He woke up every morning with apricot juice on his hands
though sometimes it was more like blood judging from
the stickiness and the telltale color, that pink,
and he just waited calmly for the cold water to boil
before he began his whispering or put on his black shoes.

He was looking at an eastern sycamore planted
in an inch of dirt although from his window seat he
could hardly see the balls and the strangulated skin.
Spring this year would come through his metal slats,
a little constrained but still wet streets and daylight

and still a wren, though out of sight, he knew her
by her gurgling, he knew her tail was up and he knew
the wind would bring her just what she needed. He could
tell the rain had stopped because the soup kettle
was barely wet, no more than a half inch of water

in over twenty-four hours. He was almost ready
to try the bridge, he thought maybe this time a cap
instead of a fedora, even if the grease of the
inner band of the other had carried him twenty-two years
back and forth. He said a good morning, he ate

his breakfast in front of the moonflowers, he half-plucked
with the left and swallowed an Everything with the right
and stretched his legs in order to loosen his cables
in front of the *Inquirer,* between two destroyed cities,
the first warm day, always laboring from scratch.

III

LIGHT

The second day of Eastern Standard
there is such a sound of bird croaking
it must be either blue jay whelps
or stiff crows just barely able to gasp
after a night of rotten sleeping.

The light pours into the room
as it pours into the trees and bushes.
Either it is the confusing sun
or the confusing government—
I can't tell one from the other.

We are all in it together,
I and the crows and the blue jays,
probably cardinals too
with their demented black eyes,
hating our dreams all alike,

they with their bird dreams sighing
and sobbing in the limbs, probably
dreams of hunger brought on by
the confusion, I with the dream
I'm best at, gnawing first one bone

and then another—to my disgrace
I have to do it twice. I was
first in a cellar seducing
the wife of one friend, a redhead—
at least in the dream she was that—

her true hair is black with gray streaks—
and then I was driving another wife
to a department store in Newark, New Jersey,
from my stone house in Pennsylvania
where she got lost looking for

a clerk with a key and I grew
wounded and anxious, complications
piled on each other, boring threads
from my own life, ridiculous secrets
I was revealing to myself,

the loss of a wool bathrobe, the useless
display of my first book
behind a locked glass cabinet,
friendships ruined, familiar
surprises and new defections,

when I was battered by daylight
coming in through the two windows,
not to mention scampering,
while a red aster bled
into its yellow petals

and a crimson leaf kicked up
first a cry and then a protest
in the life of no letup and no mercy,
I and the other species,
one of us shameless and adored.

THE SORROWS

I was outside on the street picking up a
plum tomato when I remembered the vile
Moroccan in Paris and how we argued over
his oranges. I remember Gilbert was shocked
when I turned the cart over and oranges rolled
down the sidewalk—into the street. I wanted
to make it up to him for years; I felt
ashamed whenever I saw him. Here I am
forty years later on my knees on First
Avenue, maybe paying for that, or maybe
paying for my grandfather's sin, eating
a pear on Yom Kippur, burying the core
underneath the hats or towels or in
the starch and cleanser—garbage clung to it
and it grew black and withered, a withered mouse
behind the Brillo; or maybe I am only
paying for a broken bag. This is
a good position to be in, you can wrestle
with your own elbow beside a hubcap, you
can look at a piece of glass or scratch a tire
and dust your knee as you get up—in my case
it was the left. I rise from the ground with pleasure
and walk back to the fruit store for a fresh
bag. I think the strawberries are out;
I'll spread them in my sink and cut away
the black flesh and the yellow; a kind of blood
will stick to my fingers; I was born for that,
cleaning and scrubbing my hands. I pick up a cabbage,
it is the size of a mushball; where I come from
larger than a softball, except a mushball

was truly soft, unlike the rock we called
by its soothing name. I pitch it into the wall—
I can't help it—I pick it up and pitch it
one more time, it takes two pitches to ruin
a fourteen-inch cabbage. I am willing to pay
or I am willing to buy another pound
of strawberries or yellow peppers, even
pay through the nose if I have to. I am practicing
concentration now, it means a kind
of severance, but I have known about that
since I was twenty-three; it means you sit
beside another weed and watch it crack
another sidewalk. I would like to talk
to my Moroccan again. I mean I would like
to polish the oranges. Is that enough? I know
I could make him believe me! I was drunk
with laughter when I picked up the cabbage. It was
a way of falling. It is falling I think of
whenever I think of laughing, although some falling
could be so sudden those who laugh will catch
themselves in midair. "Are you hurt?" they'll say,
and reach down for an arm, or hand. My worst
fall in years was in my city, somewhere
downtown; I lay in pain and waited to see
what was broken; my glasses were lost, my hands
were burning. There was a crowd in seconds; a man
losing his balance, or tripping, is so exotic—
and terrifying. I had no time to suffer
or lie on my back and look at the sun; they picked
me up like a wet cat. If the oranges falling
shocked the Moroccan, if my laughing angered him,
he could have laughed at me when I was falling
or squeezed some juice on my forehead, I owe him that—
it was so mild in Paris then, Algerians

smoking, Rumanians dreaming of war, that lonely
Hungarian wanting to marry me so she could
come to America, her girlfriend slashing her wrists
once a month, her girlfriend's lover—Peter—
lecturing me on innocence, our trip
to Prades to hear Pablo Casals break
his vow of silence, the day in Avignon
behind a beaded doorway, my afternoon rides
to Goldenberg's to sell American typewriters
and ten-dollar bills and green passports—I was
a gangster then. I was innocent,
but not as Peter thought; I was violent
about it; it was knowledge I lacked, it was
understanding; I had to spend my lifetime
studying it, but that's not bad; my only
pleasure was understanding, just as my only
sorrow was the darkness—my wisdom would be
loving the sorrow. The oranges would have rolled
into the river, I think, if I didn't run
to catch them; Gilbert too; he ran like a squirrel
or a rabbit, hopping and jerking, a jackrabbit,
running after oranges on the Quai
d'Orsay—though it was the two of us running,
a crow and a rabbit, both from Pittsburgh, one
the grandson of a sharecropper, one
the grandson of a Polish rabbi, chasing
the gold, calming down a stunned North African,
living in such luxury, in such sorrows.

PROGRESS AND POVERTY

In the days of Henry George
I was, like anyone else, a lover of ground rent,
and carried his book for just a little while
against my upper chest, like a leather Bible.

I wanted equal rights to the soil
though I owned practically nothing
and read all day and night
for the sake of justice and prosperity.

My room was never dark
because of the light across the way
so morning and evening were always the same
as far as working—and sleeping—were concerned.

I was for love more than equal distribution
and longed for upstate New York
or central Pennsylvania, the Blue Mountains.
I went to work too soon

Progress and Poverty, by Henry George, was a bible to young idealists in the
first decades of the twentieth century. Its central idea was that unused land
alone should be taxed and that this would bring equality and justice. George
was an inspirational reformer, in the age of reform, a famous radical, and ran
for mayor of New York City in 1886, beating out the Republican, Theodore
Roosevelt, and losing by a few votes to the "boughten" Democrat. I read him
when I was eighteen or nineteen, along with any other visionary, religious or
political, sane or otherwise, I could get my hands on.

and lost my balance a little in the shuffle.
I long to understand
and I'm not sure but I think I was enraged
too early; I like to think it was the mountains

that shut off knowledge, or it was obedience,
the sickness of my city and the sickness
of my own life, or call it terror or just
embarrassment—it took me the second half

to recover. I believed in the new kites
and ran from Wildwood to Atlantic City
with all those birds in my hand;
but I also believed in sitting in the sand

tying rags together. And I believed
in something motionless, something almost unbroken,
although for now I am not sure—I think
I *called* it perfection—I used that word—I read with

an exploding heart, an exploding mind,
but there was another side, I lived to the west
of the Alleghenies and what was darkness was always
for me a godsend, for I had time to practice

my slowness and stubbornness. My very first car
I bought for a quarter, a scheme to outwit the six
percent sales tax and make the magistrates shiver.
It was a 1950 Chevy—I bought it

in 1959; I was already
in my middle thirties and I had been practicing
for almost fifteen years. I drove my daughter
every day to see a mechanical cow

on a billboard and I bought seven pounds of lamb
for a dollar, mostly bones, and good for one
good meal. I guess by then I had left the land
but I was still loyal, I was stubborn, I clung to

New York and Pennsylvania: it was something
I think my father had said; it was the cheese
they made in Russia; it was the root beer my grandmother
made in Homestead, and it was the light that burned

both day and night; I read by that light; I lived
beside an open airshaft with a bathroom
down the hall. It was starkness I wanted,
and true separation; it was libraries

and free music and complex marriage and sadness
lived in the open. It was renunciation.
But it was memory too, and musing. It was
watching myself explode, it was exploding.

HIS CUP

His song was only a dot—a flash—if anything,
somewhere above that haze which he remembered,
when he thought about it, as a world on fire
or a white mind watching. When he shook his cup
there was a tremor, something like a distant
coruscation, he knew this and his own mind
was always either on that or on the sky
north of his grandmother's house and the long building
they called the forge and the 1939 Chevy
with the gray metal visor and the sweet acorn
with the spiked helmet. He remembered a pig
burning in sand and how they hunted all day
for the two hot eyes, and he remembered floating
under the wire they stretched across the creek
and holding his breath. The violin star is closest,
the trombone star is farthest—or the drum star—
depending on what he sang. He worked this out,
some ratio or other, forty years ago
in order to learn how music worked. If there
was an analogue for what he did it was a
nova exploding in front of the Chemical Bank,
a state of mind of the millionth brightness, his cup
gone wild, the light spilling—nothing
could take that from him. He ate from a leather case
and slept where he worked; he put quarters in one pocket
and dimes in another. As far as a change of belief,
as far as the red and the blue, as far as abortion
and standing armies and cheaper health care, even as
far as the final outburst, he was silent—
dumb, you'd say—that was the evil of music

as well as the good; and twice he changed his corner,
and once he left his cup where it was and started
howling, what else could you call it? Moaning,
hissing even, such was the light there and such
was the uncreated light. He ended up
somewhere between a rubbing and scraping, maybe
a kind of sucking, but mostly he plucked, for plucking
was how he explained it, he was both singing and plucking
and dust and gasses were collecting for he was
thinking of something else, oh, prairie schooners
fording the creek, the raging channel against
the farther side; and justice again, that which
confounded it from the beginning, and he was
dying to taste those pork chops and walk the fences
between the cows, and he was dying to feed them
and watch them eat; and in the second brain,
for it is always the second brain that makes
the lucid sounds, or so he reasoned, he watched
himself in a black suit seated at a score
on a polished stage with pipes behind him and baffles
to the left and right, his shoes polished, the light
shining on the wood, a rapt audience
of college students in rags and older professionals
and business people ready to leap to their feet
and shout for him, but he just finished the piece
on a long slow note and waited for the last
invisible sound and then two seconds of silence
before he rose and entered that thunder, his mind
already on the next great piece, how this time
the strings would fly more and the lights would burst
without stopping, or put it this way, there would
be a desert and he would walk till the blood
was almost gone and he would be a thrasher
with only two sharp sounds, or he would play

the first instrument, something to do with slapping
and something with whistling. He was grateful to the woman
who kept applauding, he bowed to her, he did
that dumb kissing with his hand, only finding
a ratio between the two, the sound of kissing,
the sound of clapping—she would give him a dollar
if she were passing by his bank, the light
was on her and she *was* the light; like him
she made it appear and disappear, her clapping
in tune with his kissing, in an empty hall
of maybe three hundred seats—they were the last
and walked into the parking lot, a single
Plymouth was there, the moon was full, the frogs
were at it again, such melody, and such, such
gruesome rhythm—he loved all frogs—his head
was in her lap, the car was moving, the cup
was spilling again, this was his major explosion.

IV

DIRTY HANDS

Sitting under a cheap stamped early light fixture
he could imagine it was he who drove the Pontiac
all the way to Florida on only one quart of oil,
something it was impossible to explain to his new girlfriend
floating in her hot tub under a Niagara grape arbor.
He took a bite of sandwich and lived on the richness
of that dark wallpaper; he thought it was round fishes
and not just some green design made in Toledo,
the wallpaper capital of the world before the First War.
He wanted to tell her how worn out he used to be
at four in the morning crossing the empty highway
to start his second night and how he struggled
with the dirty stove so he could just move his fingers;
and he wanted to tell her what it was like lugging eggs
in the Union Station in all that smoke, his lungs
turning to stone, his hands bleeding for years,
his eyes bloodshot, but that was when he touched
her face and the moon came through the grapes, the part
where the roof didn't shade the arbor, making a valley
not so different from what he knew, two clouds
breaking off like dogs breaking off, the rabbit silent
and running with his legs on fire, it was
a memory of the sun; he thought of their mouths
all open, the grapes were hard, the water was boiling
driving through West Virginia, the oil was smoking
under the hood, his eyes were closed, his hands were soaking.

GREEK NEIGHBOR HOME
FROM THE HOSPITAL

Where he hung the bird feeder a month ago
a kind of film is covering the thin glass
and where he threw his wine glass down a bleeding heart
is starting to show under the motherly leaves.

He has walked to the wire fence three times
to study my tomatoes and he has smelled
my roses in a downward movement in which
his good leg was one anchor and his cane another.

I can tell by the clicks of triumph and the loud
rattle of his newspaper the Russians
have sold missiles to the Greek Cypriots
and Turkey is going to suffer. As I recall

he put the key to the padlock in the pot
of new lettuce and I can see his glasses
under his chair in case he panics. The wind
makes both of us smile a little and the swallows

for just a second seem to lounge, the sky
is so blue, they almost rest. He leaves his chair
by twirling; he hates their rectitude, and since
the dog is dead, and since his wife went to live

with her daughter again he closes the door by himself
and either sits in the kitchen and falls asleep
over his cane or climbs his eighteen stairs
before he turns the light on—I'll know which

by the count of thirty, either one of which,
to my way of thinking, is better than the brutal
battles they had, at least for my own sleep
over the honey locust, before his stroke

a month ago in front of the glass feeder
separating the different kinds of birdseed
into their small compartments without giving
too much away to the poisonous squirrels, poor Greek.

PENNSYLVANIA BIO

I wore a black knit hat
so I could be undistinguished in the war
and carried a small bag
so I could be mistaken for a doctor;

and once in a whorehouse
while waiting for a friend of mine to finish
I examined the madam on the kitchen table;
and I spent Sunday at either the Serbian Club

or the postwar Literary Club on Atwood Street
above the prewar clothing store, and ate
hot sausage sandwiches and cold buttermilk
across the street from the first Carnegie Library

and made plans for the next seventy years. I drove
Andy Warhol to the East Liberty train station
in my father's 1949 Ford. Believe it or
not I bought a 1949 Buick

thirteen years later for fifteen dollars and drove it
into a junkyard six years after. My first
instrument was a kind of kazoo and that led
naturally to a French trombone. I was

loyal to my own music for fifty years
though I detested snare drums and tap dancing,
just as I do those singers now who hold
their left fists in the air while holding the microphone

inside their mouths. And I hate short-sleeved shirts
when they wear them with dark neckties, skinny swine
knocking on closed doors; and I had a habit
of counting bricks, a nice obsession compared to

washing hands or touching car doors, it gave me
freedom with walls so I could handle bulging
and sagging when I had to; and one of the summers
I read Steinbeck and made love—in the bedroom—

to my aunt's cleaning woman in upstate Pennsylvania
and learned to adore the small town with its rows
of stores and trees on the sidewalk and only a short walk
into the country, in this case up a steep hill,

the dogs more sullen the farther up you went,
and Russian and Roman churches below, the sunlight
on the river, the bridge empty, the outer one
half-hidden, I was shocked by the sudden distance,

and I had a Brown's Beach jacket with a reddish
thorn in one of the pockets, which was my toothpick
for thirty-five years, and a vest to match, and a flattened
acorn I kept in the darkness; and I had a pencil

I used to keep my balance, the edges were eaten,
the lead was gray, the green eraser was worn
down to the metal, and I had a spiral notebook
I kept for emotions, and I folded my money.

MASSACHUSETTS SONG

That is the education of a tree,
one stick by which morality, aesthetics,
music, and politics are taught,
whether a pecan or plum;

and that the wire,
although I hate to mention the wire,
and reddish apples and limbs so low
they drag on the ground;

and that the confluence where
five branches start, a university
hard by the lonely peach;
and that a nest for the bluebird,

a wooden box with a hole
too small for the sparrow;
and that is the loaded branch of the pitch pine where
I saw the perfect body and heard the song

in secret oh I swear you swallows I swear
you sunlight on the salt grass what the blue jay
called silence what the rose hip
and the dead raccoon called home you crows.

Where he was the silk
was in two strands and he could pull and lift it
  according to the laws of
versatility and recompense. He could stretch it
  and it was then a harp
and it gave up more knowledge though it was harsh
  the way a harp is harsh
and like a toy piano, and when he turned it
  to the light it shone
the way a horde shines or the way a stone
  with specks of mica does.
It was called the dark years for a while
  but now he called it the future,
always a surprise, though he was carrying
  the same Montaigne and even
the same footlocker, with the same universal
  lock, only it had a different
twist, his bones were truly different, he sat
  or flew now in and out
of mirrors, the brown silk fluttered, and one of the knots
  that stood for a year in France
he played with as he sat and whispered. He was
  reading the essay on cannibals
and he was doing it a second time, and he was
  standing across from the Europa
or he was in the coffee-room sinking under
  a huge chandelier and staring
at the wooden balcony and the four green plants
  in the four corners and studying

the paper money, a thin medieval king,
  an eagle with his tongue out,
a kind of nun, a kind of romantic poet,
  a kind of philosopher,
and holding the waitress, as it turned out wholly
  through political delirium,
comparing one dead rat to another, knocking
  the toothpicks over, still wiping
his head as he always did, planning a day trip
  to the south, going over his schedule,
and turning the scarf around as he walked past
  two slouching monuments,
looking to see if they were stone or metal
  and if there was any music.
The orange dots stood for Greece, since something had to,
  probably the flowers—the cheese.
The zigzag borders—the lightning—*that* stood for Broadway.
  Who would believe it? The threads
were thinnest there, the knots were hardest; he stretched it
  almost to breaking, he could
cover his whole head, he could curtsy.

A ROSE BETWEEN THE SHEETS

Taffeta for you and taffeta for me, a rose
between the sheets and one sitting on my finger
as if it were a ruben-stein; a dress
you held once in your arms against your face
and one I lifted over your waist and spread
like a noisy pillow; you in your silk and me
in my leather jacket, nothing else, raw silk
for you, cowhide for me, and velvet
on your lips, your cheek on fire, the red of the one
against the red of the other; lustrous, I'd say;
and always bright, and always florid, and ready
always to escape; your marriage for you
and mine for me, wool, wool, in my face
and cotton in my arms, a linen once I touched
with such a silly reverence, and burlap
with the loose weave, the smell of burlap, and crepe,
the way it draped, the way it absorbed the light;
and lace for romance, and corduroy for romance,
and satin for you, and satin for me, and creases
and buttons, a kind of board, I'd say, a bed,
a cushion for your ear, maybe green, maybe
gray for your hair—and blue for me, or peach—
I love the peach—a scarf for you, a scarf
for me, a white carnation for the cold,
a sunburst, a rose of Sharon for the darkness.

SWIFTS

Bing Crosby died in Spain
while playing golf with Franco
but who could care less, and at this
writing only a few of
my dear ones are gone—ah I
could make a sad list—the swifts,
as if to prove a point,
fly into the light and make
a mockery out of our darkness.
They scream for food but in
the world of shadows they only
make a quick motion; I have
studied them—the whiter
the wall is—the barer the bulb—
the more they scream, the more
they dip down. I have made
my two hands into a shape
and I have darkened the wall
to see what it looks like—I have
shortened my two broken fingers
to make the small tail and twisted
the knuckles sideways so when
they come in to eat one shadow
overtakes the other, that way
I can live in the darkness
with Franco's poisonous head
and Crosby's ears, who fainted,
a thousand to one, behind a
number six iron, though no swift
died for him, well, for them,

digging for clubs. I watch the
birds every night; they fly
in a great circle, much larger
than what I can see, their dipping
is what I dreaded in front of
my plain white wall—I say it
for the nine hundred Americans
who died in Spain. I thought
I'd have to wait forever
to do them a tiny justice
and listen to their songs
and die a little from the foolhardy
mournful notes, flying down
one air current or another
and doing the sides of buildings
and tops of trees, the low-lying
straggling dogwood, the full-bodied
large red maple, dear ones.

STREET OF THE BUTCHERS

It was called the early years in upstate Pennsylvania
or it was called the first long trek with a footlocker
up over his shoulder so he had to bend both knees
at almost every landing. He held his head
sideways, as if for listening, it was called killing
worms, the bells had already started, the second
or third, he thought; by his calculations, the ringing
would stop by the number seven. He thought maybe
almost two seconds for each long ring; he counted
himself among the chosen ones to be in the
bell's range. He knew he would lie down on his back
after he tried the faucets and opened the windows,
and go to sleep with the sound. It was called
the first concert, the bird in the iron mouth.

ABOUT WOMEN

Trying to find out about women I realized
it was glasses was the key to everything,
and watching one with huge white comic frames
belittling her nose I realized my life had passed
in ignorance.
        And when she picked her flower
and she was dragged into Hell I knew I'd have to
think about it for fifty years and sit there
on the edge of my sofa with my thick wool
melton shirt and wool socks figuring out
the path in and the path out, especially now—
more than a while ago—that I was doing
so many final things.
        Seeing her go,
or going before her, I was humiliated
first by the mud, then by the trees; and it was
morbid leaving the road for we had to walk
through almost a forest of vines; and it was foolish
being philosophical while she screamed in
my ear or cut up food in her tiny kitchen,
either holding a book near my eye or glaring
back at the sun since there was no stick to carry
or silk to tie.
        When we climbed down the hill
we hung on to the bushes, and when we walked
beside the shallow river it was her dog
made peace between us.
        It may have been only loosestrife
between the rocks, or tiger lilies; the trees
may have been ruined by too much salt, and water

may have reversed the channel unless the tide
moved it back and forth, but it was easy
going across and neither of us wanted to look
for there was only darkness, given the time
of the year, and it was cold in spite of the bright
new scarves she worked on during the summer, the orange
I always called yellow, the blue I always called green,
they were so unembellished, and how it was windy
and even noisy and how we had to yell.

LAST HOME

The name of the alley is Pine Street where the rottweiler
pushed his way into a degrading doghouse
past a filthy towel that served as a floating
door or window to keep out the light. The street
is called Walnut where there is a posted sign
and six or seven refrigerators for sale
in the front yard and two or three boarded-up windows,
and it is Fifth, I think, where I walked through
the mourners in front of the converted synagogue;
and it is one of the hills, Ferry or College,
that I climbed up to see if I could strike a
balance between my leather lung and my sodden
thigh, and which would go first and how long it took
before we could breathe on our own and whether the sycamore
that split the stone sidewalk came by the wind
a half a mile below or it was just planted
for shade and beauty. And how high you had to go
to see both bridges, and where you should stand to hear
the roar, and if you still could hear the ringing.

FORSYTHIA

At the Hill School guest house in Pottstown, PA

At seven o'clock in the morning the only reading
was a condensation of an African novel
in which an Englishwoman's faith is tested
in the rage after Lumumba's assassination;
and the only wallpaper was a bluish print of
branches and blossoms in a latticed arrangement,
giving a kind of deadly peace to the wall
and—well—a chaotic collection of dried flowers
framed and mirrored and glassed, with a piece of birch bark
in the lower right-hand corner with this message:
For Old Time's Sake, written across the lenticels.

But I was determined to watch a small bird and study
the root system of a scraggly walnut
and reach out from the second story to pick
a magnolia bud and put it in my mouth
like a Chesterfield or a Marsh Wheeling and feel
the juices run down my chin and take *something,*
a miniature hurricane lamp, a bar of soap,
back to my car and on the way confront
my first yellow bush since it was seventy degrees
and winter was gone and see what I would do
with the orange mud and the green branches this time.

LAVENDER

for Karl Stirner

Just for experiment I am burning the lavender
and scenting the air for if I only crumble it
the smell, though overwhelming, will not go
beyond a foot or two and for that matter the
stalks will hardly give off an odor whereas the
flames make everything blatant even as they
wipe out the other odors, in this case mint and
curled petunias under your French window where
I walk back and forth crying from the smoke
and moaning for the sachet I never had
and the box full of silk, I was such an enemy.

LARRY LEVIS VISITS EASTON, PA. DURING A NOVEMBER FREEZE

I said "Dear Larry" as I put down his book, *Elegy,*
across the street from the Home Energy Center

and its two embellished secular Christmas trees
and its two red wreaths over red ribbon crosses

enshrining a thirty-inch stove in one of its windows
and a fifty-gallon water heater in the other,

knowing how wise he would have been with the parking lot
and the tree that refused against all odds and all

sane agreements and codicils to let its dead leaves
for God's sake fall in some kind of trivial decency

and how he would have stopped with me always beside him
to watch a girl in a white fur parka and boots

build the first snowball on Northampton Street she collected
from the hood of a Ford Fairlane underneath that tree

and throw it she thought at a small speed-limit sign
although it landed with a fluff just shy of the twin

painted center lines inducing the three of us,
her lover, Larry, and me to make our own snowballs

from the hoods and fenders of our own Fairlanes although
she threw like none of us and to add to it

she was left-handed, so bless her, may she have
a good job and children and always be free of cancer

and may the two of us scrape some roofs before the
rain relieves us, and may we find gloves for our labor.

V

SHORT WORDS

Some dried-up phlox so old the blue was white
and something like a fireweed and grass
hopeful as always and I with a poison berry
I wanted to eat and make it my morning cracker,
and coffee so sweet I knew I put a sugar
substitute into my cup and milk so sweet
it might have been Carnation, and there was wind,
whether it was the rain coming in or only
a little cleanliness, and in the burn pile
a dead and rusty pine tree halfway sticking
out to remind me of the 1950 Buick
Mike Levey gave me in 1963
and I drove five years later into a junkyard,
and how I lost two jobs and almost three
because I was a little like Amos and longed
only to hear short words and one day a whole
student body waited in the parking lot
while I walked in alone to get my letter
of intent from a nervous college president
with pink fingernails and shaking fingers;
and who was it climbed the six-foot wall by himself
in order to teach his classes the Board of Idiots
at Temple University erected to keep
the Negroes out, and who is still ashamed
after fifty years he turned away from his first
loyalty because someone misspelled a word
or didn't speak French or never had stood with his hand
under his chin supporting the elbow with one
middle finger in front of a gorgeous old
Simone Martini painted on mountain pine;

and this is what Amos taught, that you should rebuke
all liars, straddlers, and accommodators,
all paper rats, all priests with castanets,
and all their scoffing, indifference and silence,
that you should obstruct them and even intervene,
and you should remove the wall and you should grow
your own lilac and you should kiss on the mouth;
dried-out marsh grass, dead lilies, August roses.

THE MUSIC

He is not the only one getting ready only
I insist there is more to it than singing your
black heart out or missing some ruts in a road
to Wheeling, West Virginia, how you bounced then
and how you went back again and again to find
the bush that almost choked you and the house
with upper windows blistering in the sunlight
for there is a debt and something still undetermined,
like curls you still remember or a brook
turned red the length of the stretch between the bridges,
and you decide whether it's rust from Such and Such
Chemical or blood from sheep or human
blood with song after song making a froth
you can't resist, and rolling up your pant leg
your toes just tingle from the music, this is
getting ready too, and if you stay too
long you still have the night to turn around in,
which I have decided is a courtroom, witnesses
screaming left and right, lawyers choking on
each other's words and, holding a hammer, Miss Just,
in robes no less, her hair cut short, an American
flag at her shoulder and a look called wisdom,
very severe; and I have decided to walk
to Trenton, New Jersey, just for the hell of it. "Trenton
makes, the world takes"; for only three dollars
I can go from Trenton to Philadelphia
through the abandoned corridor and reach
the Thirtieth Street Station, full of the morning, sunlight
pouring through the windows, pigeons inside the
waiting room, pigeons eating from napkins,

81

and pigeons sitting on the benches. I have
decided to walk on Chestnut instead of Market,
and I have decided not to wait for the snow
and the dog's desperate breathing, and I have decided
not to change for you, rigid lover.

NIGHT

If only the bell keeps him alive though that is
an odd way of looking at his new life, then
missing an hour because of sleep or guessing the
time and being off sometimes for two hours
won't be his undoing, not that alone, though it is
hard to attach yourself to a new lover
and learn how she smooths her dress down or listens
to some kind of voice there or to her own silence
which he also listens to hour after hour,
sometimes lying there so long he thinks the cat
has got her tongue or that the electricity
has stopped, as in a flood, though he says to
himself there has to be another system, a
backup generator slow to crank up, he can even
hear the bell slurring, or dragging, a different sound
but reassuring nonetheless, oh more than
that, a gift in his six-hour crisis, a melodic
stroking, it is new to him, and hearing it when
it is dark and he is freezing, though pleasantly,
but lying awake, and guessing, he sometimes gets it
right on the hour, but sometimes night has just started,
the drunks are only coming home and he has
four or five more hours, the sound is brief,
forbidding, harsh, indifferent, and he is surprised that
he has guessed wrong, a voice has wounded him, wind
has slammed his window shut or his door but he
just lies on his back and even opens his eyes
in the dark, for that is a life too, and he turns
to one side or the other and hangs onto something,
a chair, a windowsill, and waits for the next
shocking stroke and sometimes he changes pillows.

DROWNING ON THE PAMET RIVER

Because of the pull I ended up swimming in the grasses
a hundred yards from nowhere my beloveds
ready to jump in after me a black willow
rushing in to save me—my kind of dolphin—you
think I struggled a yard at a time but I was
nudged a little that's why my lips were red
instead of blue that's why I had the words
to "The Dipsey Doodle" still on my tongue and I was
waltzing under your huge white towel your bathrobe
over my head hot tea already burning
my throat that's why I loved the two Labradors
so much that's why I kissed you so desperately.

ART

When he died, or when he was thinking of dying,
though he hated to mention it to his former wife,
it made her so nervous, it made the cat so jumpy,
he was sitting, he said, with his friend Norman
singing songs from southern West Virginia
and going through an early flip book over and over
starring Jack Oakie and Alice Faye. They were,
he said, the B movie stars of his youth; Jack Oakie,
he said, did theater before he came to Hollywood,
some Shaw, some Ibsen, and he played Titus in
a college production of *Titus Andronicus*
which marked him forever. Alice Faye was wearing
a tight wool sweater over a pointed bra
and green lipstick. It was terrible to die
with your mind on the thirties, flipping through erotica
and singing in a kind of half-falsetto,
though that is where he chose to be or even
that is just where he was. Norman's shoes
were size fourteen, his cheeks were blue, they sang
a prison song and moaned together, Norman
went on for an hour, *that* was dying, something
like a lightbulb shone on them, something like a whistle
woke them up, they made their beds, just as
dawn was breaking in West Virginia, there was
no place to shit alone, though not one song
mentions it. A swallow came by. It made
a motion on the wall. The light of the sun,
as I understand it, creates the darkness, a way
of saying that life brings death, both he and Norman

creates his opposite

drank to that, for him a Rolling Rock,
for Norman a cup of tea; they drank, he said,
to the shadow, they drank to Titus, blood frothing
in their empty mouths, their arms just stumps they wrapped
their sweaters over, they drank to the thirties, a swallow
led the way, she dove for something ignominious
but on the wall it was a tender motion
and, after all, they were just shadows themselves
and shaking and skipping, for one of them played with strings
and one of them pounded on something flat; they kept
the old erotica in a paper bag and
one of them waved his arms to imitate
the shadow, it had to be the Rolling Rock,
the tea was too big and slow, he practiced swooping,
he practiced holding his wing to his chest, he died
slowly, an inch at a time, and he died quickly,
a kind of drop or fall, and there was a roar
of applause, I think an engine was racing nearby
for it was the thirties, remember, and we lived close
to factories then; he knew it at once when the swallow
began her drop, it was already in his mind.

MEXICAN
for A. M. M.

By holding the mirror above my head your face
was tilted just enough so that the light
came in between the window and the tree
and half the clouds were shining and by twisting
one way then the other first the rays,
though beaten into the tin, half rose above
the painted bricks as if they came from your eyes
and not the other way around and second
your hair changed color since there was red somewhere
and light was the cause, although there were my wrinkles
and there was my stubble since it was already morning,
but when it came to that, by turning the mirror
a little one way half my face was in shadow
and there was a shadow under the tree, a classic
tree shadow, perfect for robins tearing those
living worms apart—if it were April and
there was some air in the ground; and we were looking
ravenous and whimsical, your right hand
was on my shoulder and we were struggling a little
to hold the mirror straight, for topping it off
there was a vertical on either side and
they were on hinges, we could close them like doors
and cover up the center glass or we could
move them back and forth and get a triple
or even quadruple image, we could grieve
three or four times at once and we could kiss
for hours if we held the doors just so,
and it was a kind of relief that we would miss
the lavender rising over the city—you would
call it purple anyhow, you would fight me

on blues, I know—and it was almost a pleasure
that we would miss the thaw, the river rising
and fog and pneumonia and gardens turning red
in the wrong season and ice melting and mud
wherever we walked and lightning storms without
the sound of thunder as if we were deaf and nights
so warm the phoebes were terrified and titmice
were starting to hunt for grasses while we made love.

PARIS

As I recall the meal I ate was liver
with mashed potatoes, and out of simple courtesy
I kept what I could in my briefcase or half hidden
under the table; I think an Underwood brought me
two months free living and the Polish architect
I sold it to whose teeth the Germans had smashed
at Auschwitz it gave him seven months at least,
depending on other forces. The whole thing
lasted maybe a year for by my reckoning
when I was ready to leave the stores were already
full of new things and they were cleaning the bridges
and polishing the squares. My own time
was somewhere between the Ordeal and the Recovery,
but there was food enough. The one thing
I remember about him we had the same
name in Hebrew though I don't know what he was called
in Polish—I hope not Gerald—we always walked
after lunch and stopped for coffee. By my
reckoning he was in his forties. I went
to Italy on that money, it was my first
grant, a little hopeless by later standards,
but that only made it easier to practice
deprivation—in one or two years—ketchup
with beans, seven pounds of lamb for a dollar,
bread eight cents a loaf. It was
more loyal that way, I was so stubborn I did it
ten years too long, maybe twenty, it was
my only belief, what I went there for.

ALREADY APRIL

The second day in a row I watched the same
untrimmed drooping woody forsythia
for I was thinking of getting ready, though this time
I couldn't find the shirt I wanted or even
one dry chair to sit on though I found
a violet for my hair for I was lucky,
counting the first ten houses south of the creek,
and no one had a stump that huge and yellow
poison frothing like that and white moths drowning
in what they thought was soup, and no one studied
the obituaries like that or scattered petals
when he walked through the geese and calmed them down
by talking to the bowlegged guards and whispering
something from before the war half almost
joyous half ironic given the fact that
it was already April and no one I loved had
died since early November and this year the bush
turned yellow much too soon, it was so hot
so early, I almost felt cheated, the zone I'm in,
north of Trenton and south of Allentown,
I had been so ashamed and outmaneuvered.

The hat he bought in 1949 for
fifty cents, he knew it for sure, the scarf
in 1950, for fourteen cents, he planted
his beans three inches apart, two inches deep,
and put a worm in every two holes for he was
giving back and for this purpose he carried
a twenty-ounce can without a label though it had
probably housed asparagus tips or even
French-cut beans itself, and that should be coming
full cycle, and he would get on his knees for that and
let the water take him where it had to, he
was where he wanted to be, his shirt cost a quarter,
his pants cost eighty cents, but that was before
the legs were covered with mud; the can was rusty
and both of his hands were red, he was on a hill
down from the cheap mulberry, the birch
was in a corner by itself, his shoulder
was getting tender but he had fifty more worms
to go—or a hundred—he used a stick and he would
stay there at least an hour—swelling or no swelling—
and he would finish his scraping, God or no God.

THE DOVE'S NECK

The dove's neck is so thin
and his head so small he almost
disappears like a turtle when
he turns round to stare
but he goes up to sleep
and he comes down to eat
and he can see my lavender
from where he does it though he has
no fear of the bees, I think,
who curl around the flowers
and fly from one to the other
only to eat, not sleep,
and carry the food on their backs;
but I would lie in lavender
if I had the chance, I have
already lain in alfalfa,
once in tupelo and in
western Pennsylvania in Clarion County
I lay in a field of clover and daisies almost
free for once of envy
as if my neck were also
thin and my head like a turtle's,
though he should envy me, that
sex-idiot, I who lay there
for almost an hour, practically
sleeping, a short drive east
of Ohio, near the abandoned
coal mines, half a century
after the grass had hidden
the disgusting earth including,

fair or not fair, the anger,
for all I knew, underneath that
field which seemed to tilt
in such a way that stretching
my arms and legs the flowers were
always there and the wind
was always blowing, one of
my bitter personal heavens.

SLEEP

When night comes and the swallows stop diving
I'll walk down to the chain-link fence and try
something that will surprise them, either the words
in Spanish or the melody a Polish I
learned from Libby while she was making root beer.

There was a sulphur when I was a boy and I could
taste it while walking up my hill and only
one thing more is beautiful and that's the
flashes that come without a sound for I was
seeing not only the buildings but the spaces
behind them, it was merciful. My yard

is cut in two by a wire, I have studied it
to see if it's phone or cable, I am too rich now
to tear it down, or too forgiving, the belly
is only ten feet above the lavender, I will
surprise the lavender too, my way is bending
with both legs straight, almost a type of bowing
and one arm out for balance, the Chinese mint
is taking over but how do I cut it? The flowers
are tiny and blue, the daisies are huge and white,
my tea is already cold, the moths are drowning.

AUGUST 20—21

In the age of loosestrife
a man walked down then up on the waterway
overwhelmed by the basic weeds in August which
having their last chance they stopped disguising
and flowered one more time he thought though he
may just as well have been thinking of the briefcase,
the first time in six or seven years,
and what it had inside as well as the smoothness
since it was calfskin and a gift from his son
to boot, which broke his heart, and past two small
roses of Sharon, one of the plants which gave him
endless pleasure, ridiculously on the bank of
the waterway as if they somehow were wild,
and weeds to boot, though he knew where they came from and
where the mother was planted, he had walked there so
much and by the color of the flower he
could identify it too exactly the same as
the one up north, exactly the same as the one
behind his outhouse in central Pennsylvania, though
they came in purple too, they must have been planted
to hold the soil down, to give some color, for
now he realized how far what he called the mother was
planted, near some locusts, near an iron fence,
and one of the locusts was eighty feet high, the trunk
was covered with poison ivy almost as far as
the first fork, and on his way back he stopped
by the dusty cornflowers for he was beleaguered and only
blue could help him though they were almost dead,
the way they get, and he was worn out and had to
force himself a little when he got up

from his chair, he found himself rocking for leverage,
it was a kind of joke, and it was funny, the
flag next door, a striped green and brown disc,
and next to that, two houses down, a faded
American, with fifty states, all those who
live near rivers display their flags, it is
the jauntiness, not the patriotism, he has
lost so many things, now he is losing
souls, the *New York Times* keeps track of that,
here is the carrot, here is the snowflake ragweed
he hung on another fork, it is weird that
one day it's in the business section, one day
it's in The Metro, here he is strewing his sage
and here he is strewing his coneflower, there's a daisy
and he doesn't know what it stands for though he strews it
more than he does the others, everyone has
his own water, sore decayer, he stands
above the spillway and he walks back as he did
a thousand times, the pain is in his knee,
he loves the wetness, he hates the violent sneezing.

THIS LIFE
for A. M. M.

Mostly I opened my napkin with a flair
and held my two hands neatly in my lap
or tapped the spoon as if I were deep in thought,
and once or twice I worked on a small fish
until the bones were free of almost everything
resembling this life for I was against corruption
of any kind and I ate pears and apples
until I almost exploded, and on my way
to Sarah Lawrence College in early September,
1997, I broke a white cloud in
half, through one of my open windows and watched
it change two times before I was over the bridge,
struggling to see in my mirror, and I would have given
you your half except it was gone in a minute,
just like the phlox I gave you and the rose
that turned to dust when I touched it; mostly I drove
close to the side of the road for I was careful
of all the exits and I turned at the last
second or I would have drifted through God knows what
blocks of pure Spanish with my Italian lips
looking for north and slowing down my guess is
at every corner and breathing a little since water
was gone from my life—or would have been gone—if I hadn't
found my exit, and I could concentrate now
on whether the petals were evenly dispersed
and whether the leaves were shiny or not and what
loves acid and what is hairy and what is lacy
and when it is good for eating and should you drink it
and if it was streaked with green or spotted with purple
and if it was sweet and vernal, the cloud I gave you.

FIRST GARDENIA

We were always lacking one string, weren't we,
and we carried the cello from place to place laughing
and crying alternately, though it did well
for what we needed, didn't it then, it sounded
like a viola and everyone had one joke to
tell, an Italian without a moustache, a Jew
without a watch, a Christian without a Bible,
and like the missing rib we surrounded it
with mythology and put it in a glass case
once we had the money to buy a museum. I

personally raged for fifty adult years
and, as my mother used to say, my blood boiled
whenever I thought of it. I was the one who
got arrested, but more than that, I was
the one who needed steam to breathe in. I had
a suffering eye, which made me wince, and an ear
which made me rant sometimes and knock the potato
chips down with all their dirty oils. Good thing
my roses were so huge and rotten, they almost
hung like balls, as I remember, more like
peonies, which someone I knew just loved
and petal by petal she dropped as if she were losing
her first gardenia. Good thing I learned to mourn.

THE JOKE

for Jeremy Musher

He was magnificent before a storm
when there were holes in the universe
for he was then a conductor and the lightning
went through his hands like water.

And he could see through fog for he was born stubborn
and he half-listened to the geese who raised
their heads at him and he was a master of mud,
the way he walked, and when he reached the bridge

the pain in his foot was gone and he was able to
stride again and give himself to the river,
and since he was double and upside down one house
hung by nothing and pigeons flew under its trees,

and one with a dewlap screamed at him, he felt
comfortable waving his stick, jabbing and huffing,
mostly at the guard, though he had pleasure
chasing babies down the bank and only

yelled when they hesitated, and he had
one short joke they gathered around to hear,
listening attentively, even, believe it,
giving up grass for a minute, the one that ends

with a loud groan and something like an explosion,
him throwing his stick, them dropping into the water
rank upon rank, him shouting in one of his tongues,
them honking in one of theirs, though he could leave them

without a word and heave his stick into
the row of watery houses, and he could walk
both under and over the bridge—depending on which
of the two skies he was in, and which of the arches

supported the pavement and the iron flowerpots,
and what the pipe was for and how many birds
could fit between the left and right couplings
and how many steps went down—if he had to.

SNOWDROP

There had to be more than one day of rain
and temperatures in the fifties, but even more
there had to be a letup for us to go out
with one umbrella between the four of us
and give up our argument for a minute
for one of us even to notice; and since she
came from one zone north of us and there was
a catch in her voice when she bent down we stopped
short in the rain to see the green unlacing
the white, of all places in zone six,
where half our ideas come from and umbrellas
are used with a vengeance; though as I remember
it was more like a cry and so loving that
I was a little jealous, and when she touched me,
and her way is a hand on the back, loverly
the way she gets, I coughed for comfort and even
the purple stones were a comfort, the way they bulge
like buttresses, and since the mournful chow,
of all the dogs that ruined our walk, only stared
and if he barked it was almost silent we had
time in between to look at the white sycamores
and balance wood with water and hate umbrellas.

Such was the uncreated light that once
I left my bench in Christopher Park beside
the cement lesbian with the heavy breasts
and walked across the street to the Monster Bar,
the space at the corner of Fourth and Grove that used to
be the best bookstore this side of Sixth,
I tripped a little on the curb turning
my head on its socket because of hair or something
someone carried, and such was my Aristotle
that when I wiped the window to look inside
by definition I was excluded and when I
walked around to the side of the building, only
it was the front now, there was Sheridan in
the standing position, across the way, a little
inaccessible and in his slouch hat
hardly the beast he was, a kind of tall
pig, Sheridan, and such was the weather we made
our Christmas lists in, in the sixties, our Santa Claus
was sweating inside his suit, and through the branches
we heard a Brandenberg Concerto, the clouds had
almost stopped, someone was speaking Polish,
and you know me, since it was a stage, I made
my own music, and since I hated sunglasses
I started to weep, and such were the two iron gates
and the Master Lock that when I walked down Seventh
I *had* to look back, there were some vines twisted into
the top rung, I almost crashed again
into a male hydrant, it takes five years
for the bone to heal, that's when you saw me leaping.

VI

LAST BLUE

You want to get the color blue right,
just drink some blue milk from a blue cup;
wait for the blue light of morning
or evening with its blue aftermath.

You want to understand,
look at the parking lines outside my window,
the neon moon outside Jabberwocky's.

And funk! You have to know funk.
A touch of blue at the base of the spine;
long threads going into your heart;
a steaming fountain you pour into your own bowl.

My dead sister's eyes!
Those of her porcelain twin at the Lambertville Flea,
twenty dollars a day for the small table,
all the merde you need to get you across the river.

And one kind of blue for a robin's egg;
and one kind of blue for a bottle of ink.
Two minds to fathom the difference.

Your earrings which as far as I can see
are there as much to play with as to look at.
Your blue pencil
which makes your eyes Egyptian. Blue bells, bluebirds,

from Austin, Texas, the dead hackster
who drank potassium, Governor Bush

who drank milk of magnesia; a chorus of saints
from Wylie Avenue and one kind of blue

for my first prayer shawl and one kind of blue for the robe
Fra Lippo gave to Mary. Blue from Mexico
and blue from Greece, that's where the difference lay
between them, in the blues; a roomful of scholars,

in Montreal one year, in New York another,
that is blue, blue was their speech, blue
were their male and female neckties, their food was blue,
their cars were rented, Christmas lights

were in the lobby, one of the bars had peanuts
in all the urns and on the upper floors
the hospitality rooms were crowded with livid
sapphire cobalt faces—I was blue

going into the tunnel, I am blue every night
at three or four o'clock; our herring was blue,
we ate it with Russian rye and boiled potatoes,
and in the summer fresh tomatoes, and coffee

mixed with sugar and milk; I sat in a chair
so close to Sonny Terry I could hear
him mumble, the criticism he made
of his own sorrow, but I was that close to Pablo

Casals in 1950, talk about blue, and
though I left it a thousand times I stood—
since I didn't have a seat—in front of an open
window of Beth Israel in Philadelphia

to hear the sobbing, such a voice, a dog
came up to me that night out of the blue
and put his muzzle in my hand nor would he
leave me for a minute, he would have stayed

with me forever and followed me up to my house
which butted onto the woods in back of the synagogue
and sat outside my door; or blue on the street
outside a Parlour near the Port Authority—

my seed inside—or blue in Ocean Grove
where sky and sea combined and walking the boardwalk
into the wind and blue in a shrink's small parking lot
watching the clock and blue in my mother's arms

always comforting her and blue with my daughter
starving herself and blue with my wife all day
playing solitaire or drawing houses and blue,
though smiling, when I came into the world, they called me

Jess Willard, thirteen pounds, and I had just hammered
Jack Dempsey into the ropes and I was shouting—
in a tinny voice—it sounded like someone weeping—
it always sounded like that—everything living.

I looked at the sun as Huxley did according
to the teachings of my cousin Eo whose name
in Pittsburgh was Israel when we were sitting on Boulevard
Raspail in order to change my vision and saw as
Huxley did the marvelous elements of the sun
including purple animals with heads like
crocodiles and tails like lions and wings that
appeared and disappeared the more I pressed my
lids or rubbed my eyes and I was wearing a
blue shirt when I leaned back and the tears
just poured down my cheeks and into the creases, Eo
at all times encouraging me and lecturing me
on vision and what it was, breaking it down
the way Huxley did and staring himself at
the sun and weeping like me, the color patches
just patches after awhile as we went back to
homunculi or sperm just swimming slowly
from west to east, in my case it always started
that way, against the stream, as it were, though I
would never stare directly, even with the thick
old glasses, though Eo was pushing me, and Huxley
would never be that mad. I did my palming
and blinking instead and taught my mind how to move,
and I remember a man who took his glass eye out
so for two blocks I put my glasses inside
one of my pockets and went without looking. I talked
to a white larva, I talked to Vasco da Gama,
I talked to Robespierre, for I could see in
one case how cruel one bastard was in velvet
pantaloons and in another how small the

severed head was, but it was after all
the sun that burned and I who walked down a filthy
stricken street in one of my stricken cities
with one hand over my eye and counted to ten
before I shifted hands and squeezed my lids
now that my glasses were off, the way I did when
I first had to stare at the harsh lights
with the door closed and saw in streaks and made the
beams that lie in objects elongate themselves
by narrowing my eyes or made them go double
just by relaxing a little and had my first
obsession then and longed to be by myself
so I could see double and I could squint and that was
the start, for me, whatever it was for Steve
Berg, blazing pages he says, or Willis
Barnstone staring all night at the Crisco sign
across the Hudson with the flashing clock
a part of the flashing firmament or Ted
Solotaroff working all winter in his father's glass shop
under a naked lightbulb, to name just three.

KINGDOM

As far as the color red
there was a splash in the southeast corner where
the tree I adored was dying.

And as for blue
it lay between the door and the first dogwood
sprawled and sucked and wilted.

And there was a definite tilt to the new apartment house
with pots of iris on the roof
and there was an indentation where a false
Italian had laid the bricks, the line was crooked
and once he got started nothing could stop him, seventy
bricks an hour, seven hundred a day.

As for daisies, I compare them to dogs
because of the commonality, I almost
want to say the loving community
as in the parks in downtown Philadelphia,
Mario Lanzo for one, Judy Garland another.

And as for the watering can,
and as for the gingko with its transitional leaf,
and as for the snapdragons, oh
I will sit and wait for that and I will
bend to pick them one by one, the red,
the orange, the mixed; and as for the railroad bridge
how long it will last,
and as for the rope hanging down from a girder, the weighted
ball a foot above the water, the life

in the river almost clearer with its simple
obscurities and new arrangements, the bushes
where they belong, inside the girders, a stray
Canada goose to swim above the cloud-stream;
and as for the bike path, how we passed each other
hugging the wall and riding on the edge,
and where we ended, either the road in front of
the billboard or the steep steps cut at an angle
below the greasy fireplace, there was—
as far as I can tell—a breaking point
and one path down and one path up,
for it was a kind of park
with grass and chains and benches
and little walkways
and fish inside a window
swimming from river to river
and I began to shiver
over my *New York Times.*

As for our touching foreheads,
and as for dancing with you and knocking books
and candlesticks on the floor,
and then our talk on Jesus, as for whether
he had a sister and whether he limped and whether he
disappeared, see Luke, and more and more
dancing, as far as that; and as for the kingdom
and what it meant in my life, how it was
sometimes like a cloud, how I used to stand
on the sidewalk and put my hand on the wall, I had
such pleasure I never wanted to move, the world
around me stopped, I think, and how I later
made my own kingdom, but I was fourteen or fifteen,
and how it wasn't what Auden thought, mere drabbles of
Sunday School Isaiah and magazine Marx but

something sweeter than that and not just bony
justice and stringy wealth, say something out of the
letters we had in the thirties, W.P.A.,
with a vengeance, nor was it kingdom come,
dying will be done, and though it would always
be later and later I loved it just as it was,
and I could smell it, it was hidden in the coal
and in the snow and in the noise the streetcars
made rounding the bend and picking up speed, I loved
walking all morning in the snow, I climbed
up icy steps thinking of how could beasts
lie down together and could the corruptible
just vanish like that, for it was a difficult climb,

and as for us, nothing was broken, only
a wine glass maybe, or an earring was lost—

and as for that, I would have broken a dish
or thrown my favorite teapot on the floor
or smashed the red and white rooster with the candy corn
feet and caramelized comb, although I would have
caressed him first since he guarded my house
and sang in an amorous voice, as far as that.